WAR

ALEX WOOLF

W

FRANKLIN WATTS
LONDON • SYDNEY

First published in Great Britain in 2023 by Hodder & Stoughton
Copyright © Hodder & Stoughton, 2023

Produced for Franklin Watts by
White-Thomson Publishing Ltd
www.wtpub.co.uk

Editor: Alex Woolf
Series Designer: Dan Prescott

HB ISBN: 978 1 4451 8746 4
PB ISBN: 978 1 4451 8747 1

Franklin Watts
An imprint of
Hachette Children's Group
Part of Hodder & Stoughton
Carmelite House
50 Victoria Embankment
London EC4Y 0DZ

An Hachette UK Company
www.hachette.co.uk
www.hachettechildrens.co.uk

MIX
Paper from
responsible sources
FSC® C104740
FSC
www.fsc.org

Printed in Dubai

Picture acknowledgements:
Alamy: US Navy Photo 5b, Wamodo 10, mark reinstein 24, Eddie Gerald 26b. Getty: Yasuyoshi Chiba/AFP 15, Turkish Red Crescent/Anadolu Agency 17b, AAREF WATAD/AFP 20, Maximilian Clarke/SOPA Images/LightRocket 23b, Guillermo Legaria/AFP 25b, Lior Mizrahi 29b. Shutterstock: RussieseO 4, Andrii Spy_k 5t, Rizvanov Ruslan 6, theerakit 7t, Everett Collection 8t, aphotostory 8b, 9t, Papipo 9b, ACHPF 11, Orlock 13, Everett Collection 14, akramalrasny 16, AlexHliv 17t, Drop of Light 18, Gojindbefs (helmet) and Michaelica (wreath) 19t, Richard Juilliart 19b, Damian Lugowski 21, Everett Collection 22, Kamila Bay 23t, ElenVD (map) and Olga Rai (dove) 25t, Talukdar David 26t, Drop of Light 27, Stephen Barnes 28, ElenVD (map) and Olga Rai (dove) 29t. Wikimedia Commons: shamsnn/Flickr 7b, Andrew Butko 12.

All design elements from Shutterstock.

The website addresses (URLs) included in this book were valid at the time of going to press. However, it is possible that contents or addresses may have changed since the publication of this book. No responsibility for any such changes can be accepted by either the author or the publisher.

All facts and statistics were correct at the time of press.

CONTENTS

WHAT ARE WAR AND CONFLICT?

The news is often full of stories of war and conflict around the world. We see pictures of damaged towns and cities, and crowds of people forced to leave their homes to avoid the violence. In this book we will look at the reasons for war and conflict, their impact on people, and what we can do to try and prevent them in the future.

Defining our terms

First, we should define what we mean by war and conflict. *War* is a state of violent hostility between nations or military groups. *Conflict* is a dispute between nations or groups, though not necessarily a violent one. Conflicts can often lead to war. The Arab-Israeli conflict (1948–present day), for example, has led to several wars.

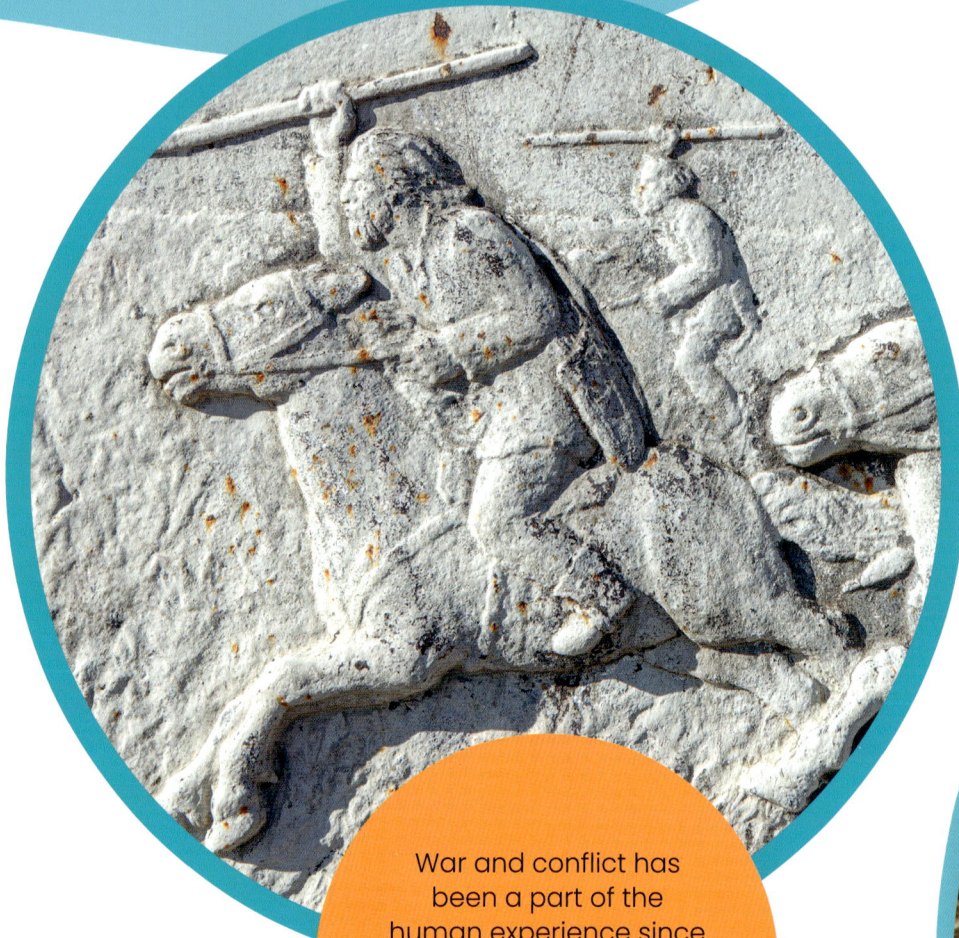

War and conflict has been a part of the human experience since ancient times. This relief shows warriors from Dacia, a Roman province from 106 to 271 or 275 CE.

Different kinds of war

Wars take many different forms. They can last years, or be over in hours. Not all wars even result in human death. In the 1859 Pig War between the United States and the United Kingdom, the only casualty was a pig.

Some wars are between two or more different nations. Others, known as civil wars, are between groups within one nation. These groups sometimes form unofficial armies called paramilitary forces or militias. These militias sometimes fight wars with more powerful national armies. This is called asymmetric warfare, or guerilla warfare.

THE HAITIAN REVOLUTION

War can occasionally bring about positive changes for those involved. In 1791, enslaved peoples in the French colony of Saint-Domingue (modern Haiti) in the Caribbean, rose up against their rulers. Their twelve-year struggle was the only successful revolt by enslaved peoples in history. The war resulted in the establishment of the independent state of Haiti, and helped inspire movements to abolish slavery.

US Army soldiers carry an American casualty to hospital following an insurgent explosion during the Iraq War in September 2007.

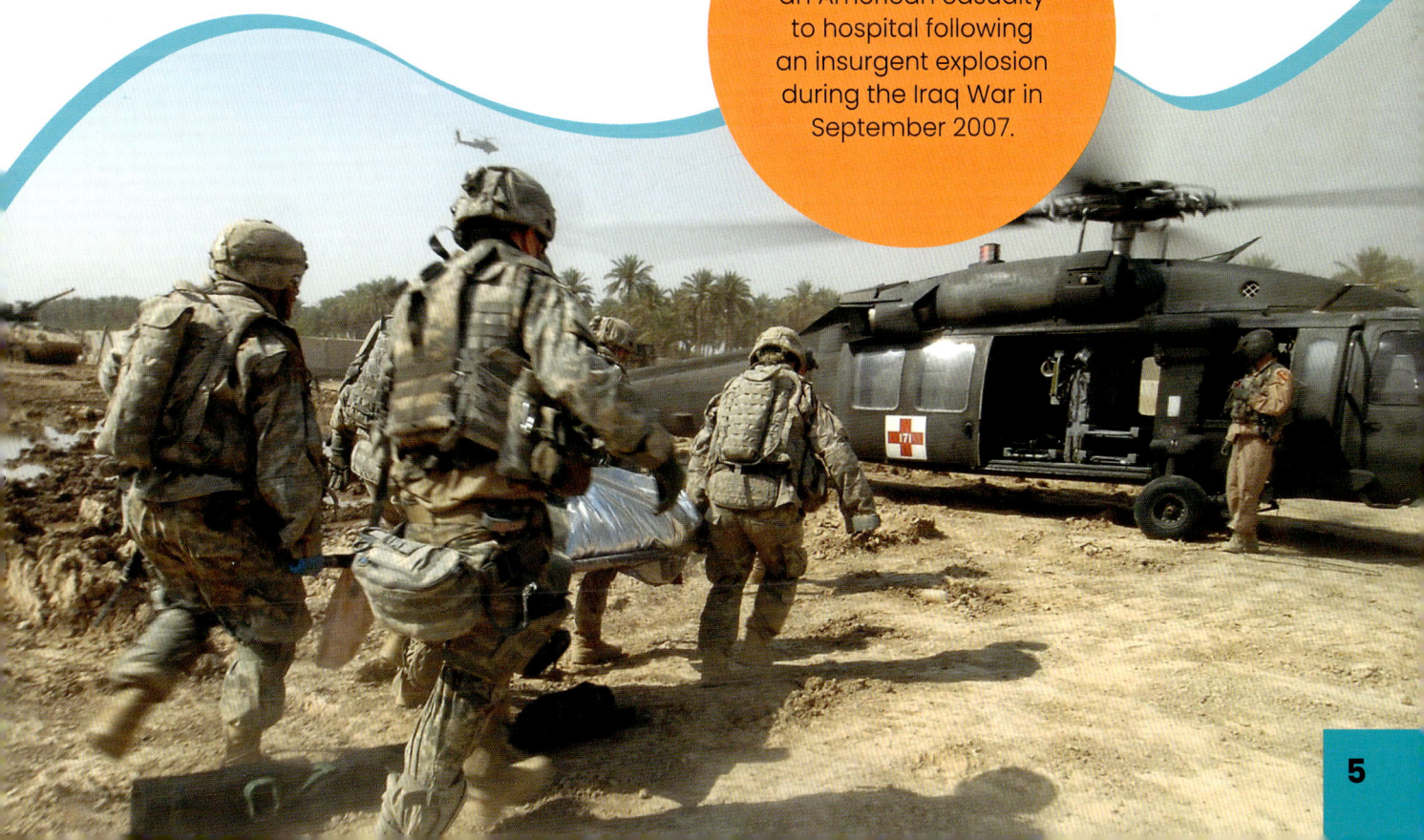

HOW WARS BREAK OUT

Just as people sometimes argue, so do nations. They – or their leaders – may argue about which of them owns a piece of land, about their rights to valuable resources, such as water or oil, or about religion. Mostly, these arguments lead to a lot of angry words. Sometimes, though, the leaders decide that the only way to get what they want is by going to war.

Attacks on nations

Wars can also start because one nation, without warning, decides to attack another. An unpopular leader may decide to start a war to gain their people's support. A powerful nation may wish to take over a weaker neighbour to make use of their resources. Or a nation may go to war out of revenge for a previous attack on them. Sometimes one nation will attack another because they see it as a threat, or fear it will attack them in the future.

Following Russia's invasion of Ukraine in February 2022, Russian forces bombarded Ukrainian cities. A rocket attack on this shopping complex in Izium left eight dead.

Civil war

Civil wars often begin because of anger against a government, or because two groups within a country attack one another. Sometimes, one of the opposing groups may wish to break away from the nation and form their own independent state. The ongoing Syrian civil war, for example, was triggered by anger against the Syrian government.

THE BREAK-UP OF YUGOSLAVIA

Sometimes war can bring benefits to a country or region. Yugoslavia was a nation containing a number of ethnic groups with different histories, beliefs and identities, creating serious political tension. When Yugoslavia broke up in 1991-2, several wars broke out. These ultimately led to the establishment of stable independent states, such as Croatia and Bosnia, each with their own ethnic identity.

A pro-democracy demonstration against the Assad government in Damascus, Syria, in April 2011.

NO FOR DISTROYING
لا للتخريب

PEACEFUL
سلمية

FIGHTING WARS

Fighting a war involves a great deal of effort and expense on the part of the nations or groups involved. Most nations have existing professional armies, but to fight a war they will usually need to recruit more soldiers. They might do this by conscripting ordinary citizens, or by paying mercenaries to fight for them. In the case of some unofficial armies, child soldiers are recruited to fight.

Munitions and infrastructure

Fighting a war requires huge resources. Armies need weapons and equipment. Factories may need to be converted to manufacture munitions. Additional defences might need to be built in case of attack, including bomb shelters, border defences and military fortifications. The armed forces will need food, shelter and transportation.

The Great Wall of China was built to defend China's northern border against invaders from the Eurasian Steppe.

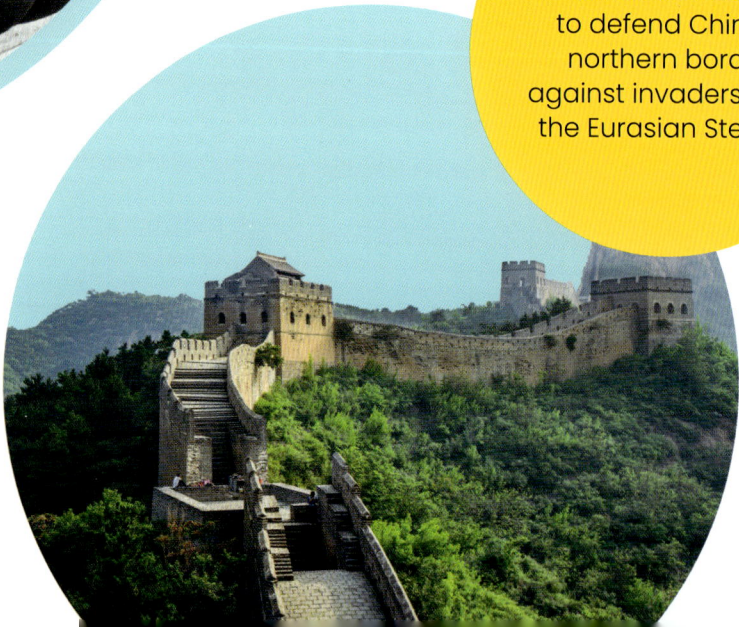

A worker checks bomb cases loaded with explosives in a munitions factory during the Second World War (1939–1945).

The costs of war

War involves sacrifice – governments may have to impose curfews and food rationing. They might have to introduce higher taxes to pay for the war effort. There is also a risk to life if towns and cities come under attack.

This poster from the First World War (1914-1918) encouraged US citizens to enlist with the armed forces.

Propaganda

Leaders intent on war must convince their citizens that, despite all the costs, war is a good idea. They use propaganda to achieve this. Propaganda is biased information that may make the enemy look bad and their own side look good in the conflict. This process of keeping up morale gets harder the longer the war drags on and the more death and suffering the civilian population endures.

PUTIN'S PROPAGANDA

During the Russia-Ukraine War, Vladimir Putin's Russian government used social media to send out pro-Russian propaganda to Ukrainian citizens. The Southern Front news site, based in the Ukrainian city of Berdansk, published misleading reports of Russian military victories, and claimed that "peaceful life" had been established in occupied areas. The Ukrainian government used fact checkers to debunk these false claims, and sent out propaganda of its own.

THE IMPACT ON SOLDIERS

On the front line of any war are the soldiers – men and women sent out to fight for their country or a particular cause. They face danger from enemy gunfire and shelling. Many of those who go off to fight do not come back. An estimated 160 million soldiers died in wars in the twentieth century.

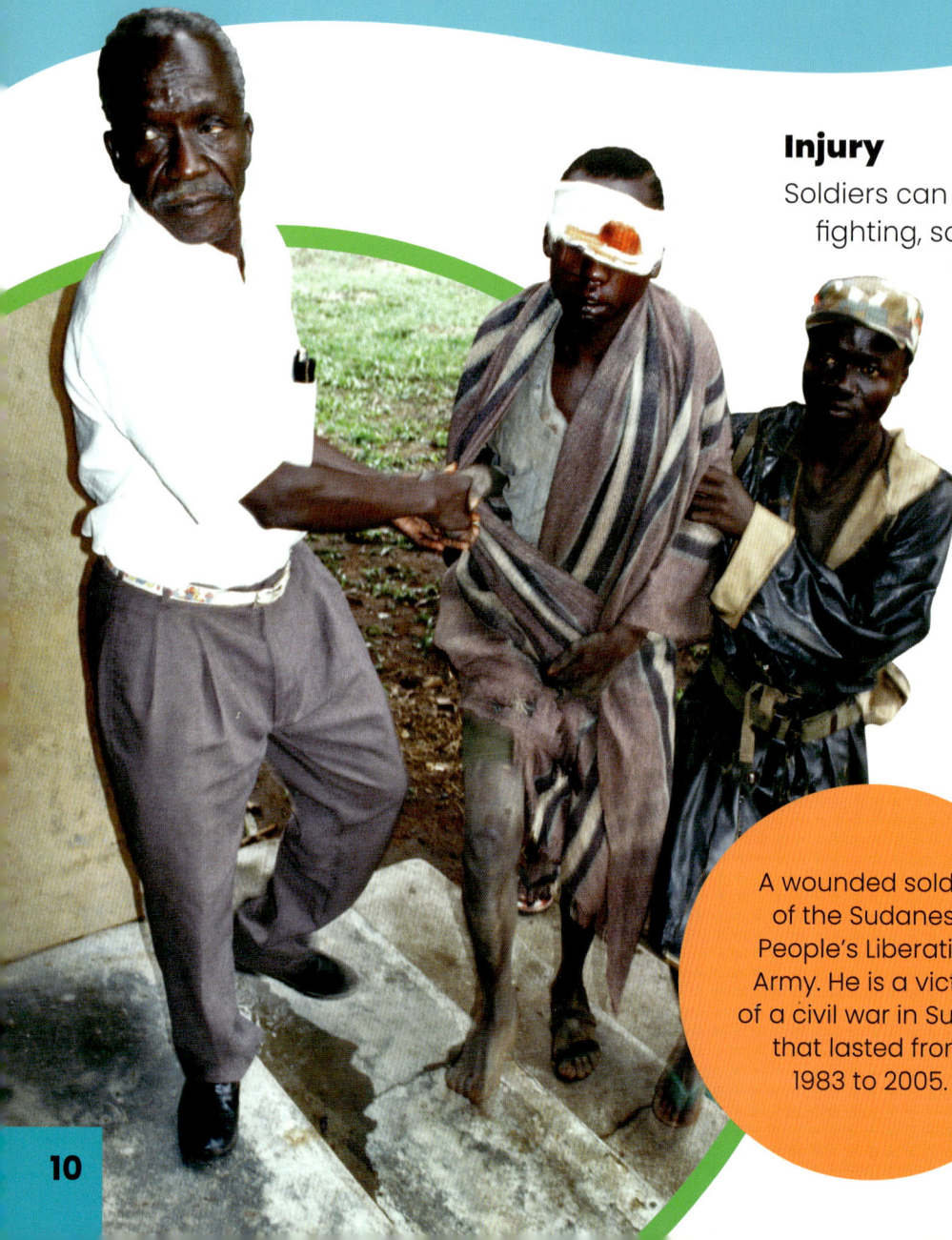

Injury

Soldiers can suffer serious injuries while fighting, some of them life-changing. Common combat injuries include burns, broken bones, shrapnel wounds and injuries to the brain, spinal cord or nerves. Soldiers may lose their sight or hearing or suffer the loss of a limb. Exposure to poisonous gases can lead to heart and lung problems.

A wounded soldier of the Sudanese People's Liberation Army. He is a victim of a civil war in Sudan that lasted from 1983 to 2005.

Mental disorders

Soldiers often undergo shocking and distressing experiences in the course of a battle. Some soldiers suffer post-traumatic stress disorder (PTSD). Symptoms can include flashbacks, nightmares, distressing thoughts and images, sweating, trembling and pain. Some former soldiers experience depression and anxiety. They may feel isolated and struggle to readjust to life after a conflict.

IT'S A FACT

Nearly 20 per cent of US soldiers – a total of 300,000 – who served in Iraq and Afghanistan reported symptoms of PTSD or serious depression.

What Can I Do?

We can all show our appreciation to military veterans by buying a poppy on Remembrance Day, which is held in many countries on 11 November. The money supports serving and ex-serving men and women and their families. There are also other kinds of remembrance ceremony around the world. In Japan, the National Memorial Service for War Dead is held each year on 2 May to remember the victims of the Second World War (1939-1945).

The Invictus Games is an international sporting event for injured servicemen and women. It was founded by Prince Harry, Duke of Sussex, in 2014. Here, athletes compete at the 2017 games in Toronto, Canada.

THE IMPACT ON CIVILIANS

A century ago, wars were mainly confined to battlefields, and soldiers were the chief casualties. That is no longer the case. Today's weapons can strike at very long ranges, putting civilians on the front line. During the First World War, just 5% of casualties were civilians. In today's wars, it can be up to 87%.

Violent deaths

People living in war zones may be killed in air raids, by gunfire, improvised explosive devices (IEDs) and by drone attack. They may be killed in their homes or in the streets. They may be shot at checkpoints, or when they step on mines. Increasingly, civilians are seen as targets by attacking forces. During the Russian invasion of Ukraine, Russian artillery and airstrikes targeted schools, hospitals and shopping centres.

A display of photos of Ukrainian civilian casualties from the Russia-Ukrainian war.

Indirect casualties

Not all civilian casualties are from direct attacks. Many deaths are a result of starvation and medical shortages caused by war. In Syria, the civil war has wrecked the country's healthcare system, leading to a decline in average life expectancy of up to twenty years. In South Sudan, nearly half a billion people suffer food insecurity due to the civil war there.

IT'S A FACT

Between 2001 and 2021, more than 387,000 civilians died in the wars in Iraq, Afghanistan, Yemen, Syria and Pakistan.

What Can I Do?

In 2019, nearly 80 million people fled their homes due to conflict. We can help refugees of war by hosting them in our homes, or by donating to or volunteering for organisations that help refugees integrate. It is very hard for someone to start a new life in a foreign country. Any small gesture of friendship you can offer will mean a great deal.

Young victims of the Syrian civil war, now living at a refugee camp in Suruc, Turkey, entertain themselves in Octobr 2015.

NUCLEAR WEAPONS

We've looked at the harm war does to the soldiers and civilians involved in it. Since the development of nuclear weapons in the 1940s, war now has the potential to harm human life all over the world.

Destructive potential

Nuclear weapons release enormous amounts of destructive energy by splitting the nucleii of atoms. In the 1950s, scientists developed the even more powerful 'hydrogen bomb' that releases energy by fusing atomic nucleii.

Nuclear weapons have the power to flatten entire cities. They also leave behind a harmful radioactive dust called fallout that can cause death and disease in survivors of the initial blast. They have been used just twice in war, when the United States dropped atomic bombs on the Japanese cities of Hiroshima and Nagasaki at the end of the Second World War (1939–1945).

The atom bomb that destroyed Nagasaki, Japan, on 9 August 1945. The mushroom cloud became the symbol of the threat of nuclear warfare.

The Cold War

During the Cold War (1945–1990), rival superpowers the United States and the Soviet Union built up vast stockpiles of nuclear weapons, as well as long-range missiles to deliver them. If a full-scale war had broken out between them, they could have unleashed enough destructive power to devastate life on Earth.

Attempts to get rid of them

Because of the devastating threat they pose, many attempts have been made over the years to rid the world of nuclear weapons. The United States and Soviet Union signed treaties to limit or reduce their nuclear arsenals. Since 1995, a total of 191 countries have signed the Treaty on the Non-Proliferation of Nuclear Weapons.

IT'S A FACT

The number of nuclear weapons in the world has been gradually declining since 1985.

1985: 63,632

1995: 39,123

2005: 26,388

2020: 13,400

Anti-nuclear weapons protesters march through Hiroshima on 6 August 2021, the anniversary of the bombing of that city.

THE RULES OF WAR

Since ancient times, people have tried to lessen the horrors of war by imposing rules on how it should be fought. Medieval Christian thinker St Thomas Aquinas said that wars should be waged in a just cause, and soldiers should avoid cruelty on the battlefield.

The Geneva Conventions

In 1864, representatives of 12 states signed the first Geneva Convention. This treaty ensured that injured soldiers on the battlefield received care. The Second Geneva Convention, adopted in 1907, covered the treatment of naval personnel. The third, in 1929, related to prisoners of war, and the fourth, adopted in 1949, protected the rights of civilians in war. The Geneva Conventions have been approved by 196 countries.

A Yemeni army soldier removes mines planted by militias in Taiz, Yemen, in 2016. The Anti-Personnel Mine Ban Treaty was adopted by the United Nations in 1997.

Enforcing the rules

Serious breaches of the Geneva Conventions, such as the killing of civilians or the torture of prisoners of war, are regarded as war crimes. Perpetrators, if caught, face arrest and trial at the International Criminal Court (ICC) in The Hague, Netherlands. Since 2002, when the ICC began operating, a number of rulers or former rulers have been charged with war crimes.

Treaties

In more recent times, countries have signed treaties establishing international standards for the conduct of war. For example, treaties have been agreed banning the use of cluster bombs, landmines and other weapons that kill indiscriminately.

RED CROSS AND RED CRESCENT

The International Red Cross and Red Crescent Movement is a humanitarian movement set up to protect victims of war and conflict. It has approximately 97 million volunteers and members worldwide. Its main aims are to ensure that governments comply with the Geneva Conventions; arrange care for wounded soldiers; supervise treatment of prisoners of war; help search for people missing in armed conflicts; and protect civilian populations in war.

A member of the Turkish Red Crescent helps a child, one of hundreds of refugees fleeing conflict in Iraq in 2016.

THE UNITED NATIONS

The United Nations (UN) was founded in 1945, at the end of the Second World War. It is an international organisation that attempts to prevent war, end conflict and maintain peace. It does this by encouraging talks between opposing sides and by sending in peacekeeping forces.

Conflict prevention

Conflict is more likely to occur in places where governments are seen as illegitimate by their people. The UN assists governments in running fair elections and helps oversee the peaceful transfer of power from one government to another. Where governments breach humanitarian laws, the UN can impose sanctions. These can include bans on trading and travel between that country and the rest of the world.

A meeting of the United Nations General Assembly in New York. Here, representatives from all 193 member states meet to discuss and agree UN policy.

Peacekeeping

The UN deploys peacekeeping forces in places where there is war or conflict. Their role is to protect civilians, reduce violence, strengthen the rule of law and promote human rights. At the same time, they help empower national authorities to take on these responsibilities when they can. Peacekeepers carry weapons but they are not supposed to use force except in self-defence or to defend the aims of their mission.

KEEPING THE PEACE IN KOSOVO

In 1998–9, Kosovo fought a successful war of independence against neighbouring Serbia. Following the war, Kosovan Serbs continued to clash with the majority Albanian population. Since June 1999, the UN has maintained a peacekeeping mission in Kosovo. Its aim is to promote security and stability and ensure conditions for a peaceful and normal life for all Kosovans.

IT'S A FACT

Since 1947, the UN has carried out 71 peacekeeping operations. The longest-running peacekeeping mission has been stationed in the Middle East since May 1948. The largest mission is in South Sudan, which involves over 19,000 personnel.

UN peacekeeping forces from Japan on patrol in Juba, South Sudan.

RESPONSES TO WAR

How should we respond when a ruler invades a neighbouring country, seizing territory and bombing cities, paying no regard to the rules of war? Most countries prefer not to intervene with military force, risking their own soldiers' lives. Instead, they try to put pressure on the invader to stop the war, and they give support to the invaded nation.

Sanctions were imposed on the Syrian government during the civil war. This man is exchanging Syrian pounds for Turkish lira because the sanctions caused an economic crisis, and the Syrian currency crashed.

Sanctions

One way to put pressure on aggressive nations is to impose sanctions. These could be bans or restrictions on trade with that country. If a nation cannot import or export goods, it suffers economically and may experience shortages of vital resources like energy and food. Ports can be closed to their ships and planes. The invading regime may have assets in foreign countries that can be seized, or accounts in foreign banks that can be 'frozen' so they cannot withdraw money from them.

Support

At the same time, countries and international organisations can offer support to the invaded nation. This can involve humanitarian assistance to civilians, including medical and food aid, emergency shelter and provision of vehicles to evacuate people from besieged areas. They may also offer military weapons, training and equipment to help them defend themselves against the invader.

What Can I Do?

We can all play our part in protesting against regimes that attack their own people or launch unprovoked wars against other countries. We can do this by joining street marches as well as raising awareness on social media. This may not, by itself, deter the invaders, but it could put pressure on our own governments to take tough action against them.

People in Warsaw, Poland, march in protest against the Russian invasion of Ukraine in February 2022.

SAFE ZONES

One way of limiting an invading nation's ability to wage war is the establishment of a military exclusion zone, also known as a safe zone. This is an area where military forces are not allowed to operate and risk being attacked if they do.

No-fly zones

When imposed in the air, these are called no-fly zones. The United States and its allies imposed no-fly zones over Iraq in 1991 to prevent the Iraqi government from attacking Kurdish people. Iraqi aircraft were forbidden from flying within these zones.

Demilitarized zone (DMZ)

This is an area where no armies or military installations are allowed. DMZs are often established along a border between two hostile powers as a means of keeping the peace. There are DMZs on the border between North and South Korea, between Iraq and Kuwait and between the northern (Turkish) and southern (Greek) parts of Cyprus.

US Air Force fighter planes patrol the no-fly zone over Iraq in 1991.

THE KOREAN DMZ

The Korean Demilitarized Zone is a strip of land 250 km long and 4 km wide dividing North and South Korea. It was established as a buffer zone following the Korean War (1950–1953) because of continuing tensions between the two countries. The DMZ is used for prisoner exchanges and attempts at peace negotiations.

Humanitarian corridors

These are temporary safe areas created in war zones to allow humanitarian aid into a region where civilians are trapped, such as a besieged city. They can also be used to transport civilians out of a dangerous area. Humanitarian corridors are very difficult to set up, and rely on the fighters on both sides to recognise them.

The UN created humanitarian corridors in 1993 in Bosnia and Herzegovina during the Bosnian War (1992–1995). In March 2022, humanitarian corridors were used to help thousands of refugees leave the besieged cities of Sumy and Mariupol in Ukraine.

Residents of Mariupol, Ukraine, flee the city through a humanitarian corridor.

TALKING PEACE

Wherever there is war and conflict, the international community will try to bring the two sides together for peace talks. The UN or a neutral country can often act as a mediator in these negotiations. The ultimate aim of peace talks is a peace treaty that will end the conflict.

The Israeli–Palestinian conflict

This conflict began in 1948 with the establishment of the state of Israel on land already inhabited by Palestinians. Since the 1970s there have been various attempts at resolving it through a peace process. In 1993, the first Oslo Accord was signed by the two sides. Norway and the United States acted as mediators. The Oslo deal collapsed by 2000 due to continued hostility and lack of trust on both sides.

The conflict endures to this day, despite attempts to restart talks. The peace process has, at least, shown the potential for a future with two states – Israel and Palestine – living peacefully side by side.

US President Bill Clinton hosts the signing of the first Oslo Accord, in September 1993, between Israeli Prime Minister Yitzhak Rabin and Palestinian leader Yasser Arafat.

Northern Ireland

In the late 1960s, a violent conflict, known as the Troubles, broke out in Northern Ireland between groups representing the Catholic-nationalist minority (who want to be united with Ireland) and the Protestant-unionist majority (who want to remain part of the UK). A peace process began in the 1990s, involving the UK, Ireland, and leaders on both sides in Northern Ireland. After prolonged negotiations, the 'Good Friday Agreement' was signed in 1998. It addressed most of the causes of the Troubles and helped forge a lasting peace.

THE COLOMBIAN PEACE PROCESS

In the 1960s, a conflict began in Colombia between a guerilla group called FARC and the Colombian government. From 1982, there were several attempts at peace talks, but they all failed. Eventually, after three years of negotiations, a peace agreement was signed in 2016. A big part of its success was the agreement of former combatants to lay down their arms and start to build a new life as peaceful citizens.

IT'S A FACT

Conflict-related deaths in Northern Ireland:
1968–1998: 3,532
1998–2018: 158

Colombians march in support of a peace agreement in October 2016.

REBUILDING TRUST

When the fighting stops, the anger and resentment that caused it doesn't always go away. Former enemies have to learn to get along and this takes a lot of work. Cities can be rebuilt; it's often harder to restore trust among people.

Disarmament

When civil wars end, former combatants must agree to lay down their weapons. This can be hard for members of militias who have grown accustomed to using violence to get their way. For it to work, former combatants must be helped to reintegrate into civilian society. Organisations like the UN can assist in the process, helping them with trauma counselling, education, training and job opportunities.

Arms laid down by former combatants are put on display.

Former child soldiers who fought for armed groups play football at a rehabilitation centre run by the UN in the Democratic Republic of Congo.

Restoring civil society

People's lives are thrown into chaos by war. Bombs destroy homes, businesses, hospitals, schools, transportation and communication networks and essential utilities. The international community can help with financial aid to rebuild countries shattered by years of conflict.

Building bridges

If peace is to last following a civil war, people also have to address the causes of the conflict and find ways of resolving it in the long term. This involves building bridges between formerly hostile communities through dialogue, and making sure that human rights are respected on both sides. This happened in Rwanda, after widespread massacres were carried out against a minority ethnic group in 1994. An organisation called Never Again Rwanda was created in 2002 to bring people from different ethnic groups to work together towards a sustainable peace.

What Can I Do?

There are many things you can do to help war-torn countries. You can donate to organisations providing life-saving humanitarian aid to victims. You can send essential items such as tents, clothing, shoes, toiletries, suitcases and toys. Write to your local political representative, asking them to welcome refugees fleeing the war. If your circumstances allow it, let them know you would be willing to host a refugee.

A volunteer distributes oatmeal to refugees in Kharkiv, Ukraine, following the invasion of their country.

A PEACEFUL FUTURE?

Conflicts occur when two groups struggle to live together. There may be a history of violence and hatred between them. Even when the fighting stops, this can leave a legacy of mutual mistrust. To overcome this, societies need to give a voice to both groups in a way that ultimately benefits everyone. One way of doing this is through power sharing.

Power sharing

Under a power-sharing system, representatives from both sides in a divided society are given leadership roles. The electoral system is designed so that the minority community always gets represented in the law-making assembly. The culture of the minority community is respected, for example by offering translations of official documents into its language.

Each community is allowed to veto laws it disapproves of. If the smaller community comprises 30 per cent of the population, then it is given 30 per cent of positions in the police force, civil service and other institutions. Power sharing has worked in divided societies such as Northern Ireland, Bosnia and Herzegovina and Lebanon.

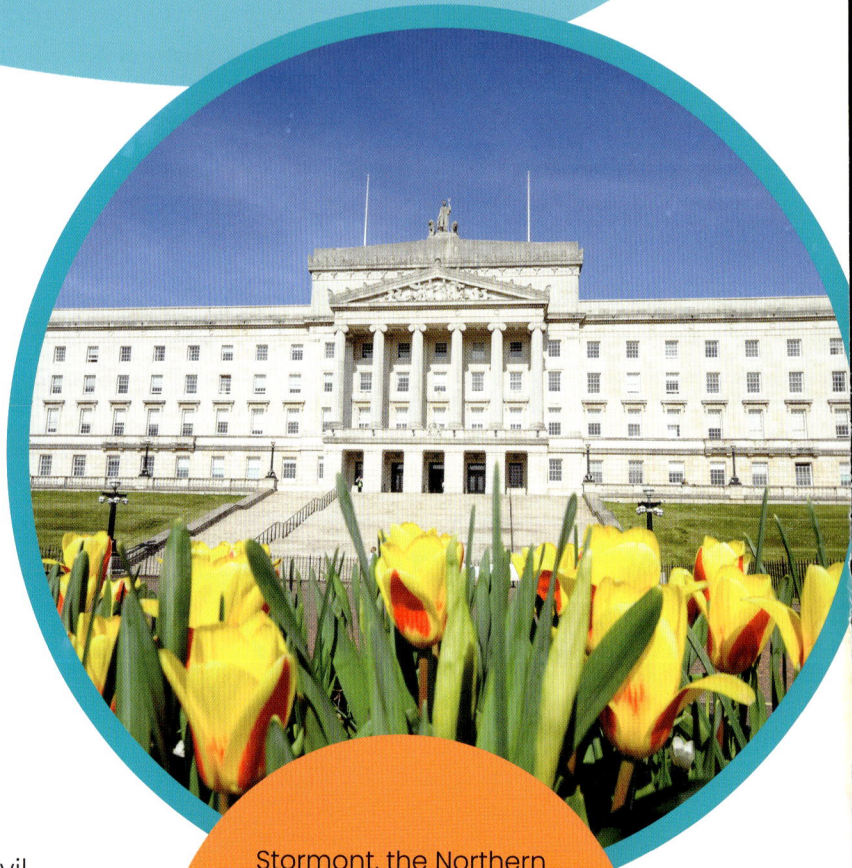

Stormont, the Northern Ireland law-making assembly. The power-sharing system here hasn't always run smoothly, and sometimes Stormont has been suspended.

Overcoming division

Another approach to creating long-term peace is to play down divisions. For example, politicians could seek to attract votes from people from both communities by offering policies that benefit everyone. Efforts can be made by schools, colleges, sports clubs and other institutions to bring in people from both communities.

In the long-term, the only way to build a peaceful, stable society is to celebrate and respect each community, and at the same time look beyond their differences to what they have in common.

THE DAYTON AGREEMENT

The Dayton Agreement was the peace deal that brought an end to the Bosnian War. It established a system in Bosnia Herzegovina whereby all three of the country's main ethnic groups – Bosniaks, Croats and Serbs – would have a share of political power.

As part of the process of building peace, Israeli conductor Daniel Barenboim leads the Palestinian Youth Orchestra in the West Bank town of Ramallah in May 2004.

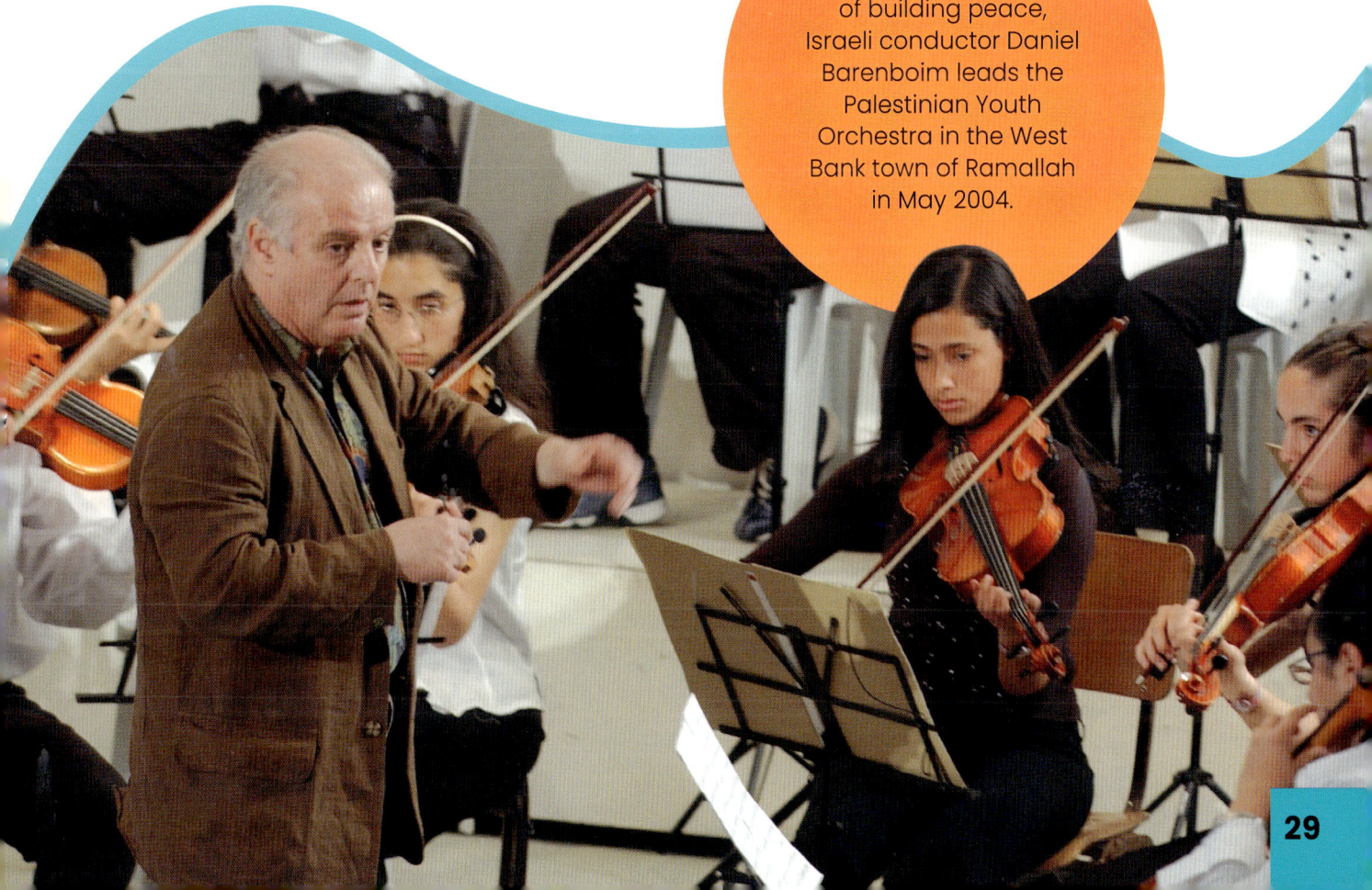

GLOSSARY

air raid An attack in which bombs are dropped from an aircraft onto a target.

arms Military weapons and equipment.

assets Items of property owned by a person or company.

casualty A person killed or injured in a war or accident.

civil war A war between citizens of the same country.

coalition A temporary alliance for combined military action.

corruption Dishonest conduct by those in power.

curfews Regulations requiring people to remain indoors during certain hours.

democracy A system in which the people of a country govern through elected representatives.

diplomacy The managing of international relations, often by a country's representatives abroad.

flashbacks Reliving traumatic events as if they're happening now.

fusing Joining or blending two or more things to make a single thing.

hostility Unfriendliness or opposition.

humanitarian Concerned with promoting human welfare.

illegitimate Not authorised by law or by consent of the people.

invasion An instance in which the forces of one country attack and try to occupy another.

life expectancy The average period that a person may expect to live.

mediation Intervention in a dispute in order to resolve it.

mercenaries Professional soldiers hired to serve in a foreign army.

munitions Military weapons, ammunition, equipment and stores.

nucleii Plural of *nucleus*, the central part of an atom

propaganda Information used to promote a political cause or point of view. Propaganda is often biased (in favour of one group and against another).

rationing A system brought in during times of shortage in which people are allowed only a fixed amount of food and other essentials.

refugee A person who has been forced to leave their country in order to escape war, persecution or natural disaster.

regime A government, especially an undemocratic one.

regime A government, especially an undemocratic one.

sanctions Measures taken by a country or countries to pressure another country into acting according to internationally accepted codes of conduct.

shrapnel Fragments of a bomb or shell thrown out by an explosion.

Soviet Union A very powerful country that occupied northern Asia and part of eastern Europe from 1922 to 1991.

treaty A formal agreement between states.

veto A right to reject a decision or proposal made by a law-making body.

FURTHER INFORMATION

Books

Children Growing Up With War by Jenny Matthews, Franklin Watts, 2016

Civil War and Genocide (Our World in Crisis) by Izzi Howell, Franklin Watts, 2018

Why do People Fight Wars by Alison Brownlie Bojang, Wayland, 2022

Websites

www.bbc.co.uk/bitesize/courses/zc3rg7h
Learn about the history of war and how it has changed through time.

www.ungeneva.org/en/un-for-kids
A website aimed at young people that explains the work of the United Nations with examples from around the world.

https://kids.britannica.com/kids/article/war/353911
A website about war, its causes and history, with links to information about different wars.

INDEX

WHAT CAN WE DO?

TITLES IN THE SERIES

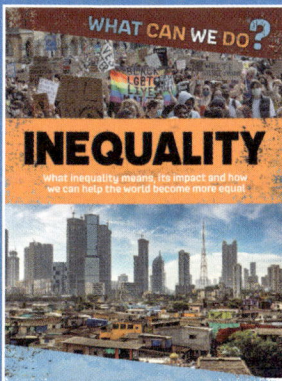

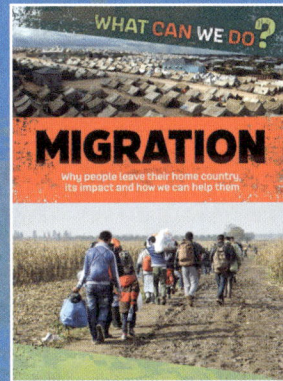

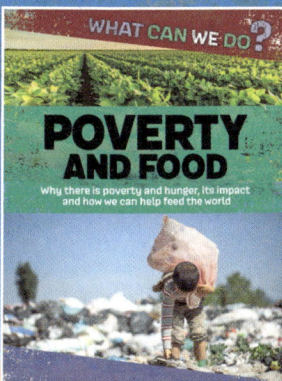

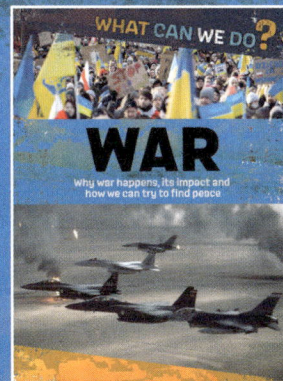